Ted's Red Sled

Written by Gary Pernick

Illustrated by Joan Holub

On Monday, Ted got red snow boots.
But it didn't snow.

On Tuesday, Ted got a red hat.
But it didn't snow.

On Wednesday, Ted got red mittens.
But it didn't snow.

On Thursday, Ted got a red sled.
But it didn't snow.

On Friday, Ted put on his red snow boots,
his red hat, and his red mittens.
But it didn't snow.

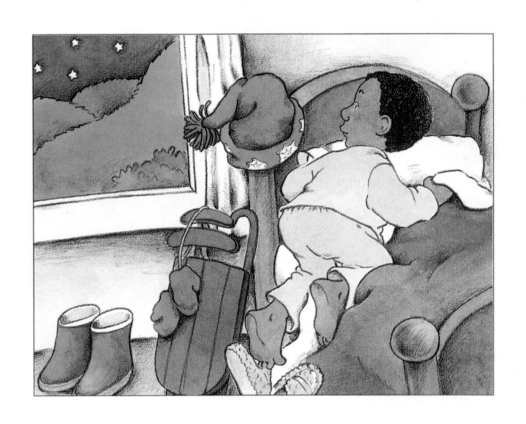

So Ted went back to bed.

8